ON THE

GENERAL THEORY

OF

PROPORTION IN ARCHITECTURAL DESIGN

AND

ITS EXEMPLIFICATION IN DETAIL IN THE PARTHENON.

WITH

ILLUSTRATIVE ENGRAVINGS.

BY W. WATKISS LLOYD.

READ AT THE ROYAL INSTITUTE OF BRITISH ARCHITECTS, JUNE 13TH, 1859.

LONDON:
JOHN WEALE, 59, HIGH HOLBORN.
1863.

This scarce antiquarian book is included in our special *Legacy Reprint Series*. In the interest of creating a more extensive selection of rare historical book reprints, we have chosen to reproduce this title even though it may possibly have occasional imperfections such as missing and blurred pages, missing text, poor pictures, markings, dark backgrounds and other reproduction issues beyond our control. Because this work is culturally important, we have made it available as a part of our commitment to protecting, preserving and promoting the world's literature. Thank you for your understanding.

INTRODUCTION.

THE course of some recent discussions touching on the history of Architecture has been incidentally modified by a certain reference to the theory that I propounded before the Institute of British Architects some years since, of the principles of architectural proportion as they were discovered and applied by the Greeks. I am, in consequence, induced to reprint the abstract of my lecture, chiefly for circulation among the members of a private Society, but willing also to make it accessible to students who are without the limited range of my personal acquaintance. The paper as reprinted here is but an abstract of the lecture, as that was of a more extended essay,—an essay, indeed, which has since grown under my hands to completion as a detailed and formal treatise. The engravings which now accompany the abstract were prepared by me when I had in view to print the essay at large. It was, however, in returning to the subject with this purpose that I became aware of new applications and natural developments of the theory, so extensive as to lead me into investigations which transformed the essay into the treatise. In this form, the project of publication became much more unmanageable. These are scarcely the days, at least this is not the country, in which at the present time the illustrator of classical architecture is in the way to find either the stimulant incitement of emulation or more than the rarest sympathetic cheer; yet without this help the labour we delight in flags and fails invariably with the many, and even with the few when the point is arrived at, where to the sacrifice of leisure hours are to be added those of the peculiar solace and immunities that wait upon secluded study.

Rejecting, therefore, any middle course, I have reverted to the reprint of the abstracted lecture. I will only say, for the encouragement of those who may become interested in the subject hereafter or elsewhere, that if they hold by the clue they may, to my certain knowledge, follow the theory into many an unexpected development, and be led to many happy and available applications; and they have my best wishes for success. Beyond this, I will leave the results now given to speak for themselves, knowing well that they who can best appreciate the condition in which I found the subject will not fail to recognise the value of the stage to which I pretend to have advanced, and where I now, with whatever reluctance, leave it.

I have disserted elsewhere on the significance of the Parthenon and its plastic adornments as a poetical and religious expression; the following are the references:—

Explanation of the Groups in the Western Pediment of the Parthenon (The Classical Museum, XVIII. 1847).

On the central Group of the Panathenaic frieze (Transactions of the Royal Society of Literature, Vol. V., new series, 1854).

On the Sculptures in the Eastern Pediment of the Parthenon (Transactions of the Royal Society of Literature, Vol. VII., new series, 1862).

W. WATKISS LLOYD.

ON THE

GENERAL THEORY

OF

PROPORTION IN ARCHITECTURAL DESIGN

AND

ITS EXEMPLIFICATION IN DETAIL IN THE PARTHENON.

READ AT THE ROYAL INSTITUTE OF BRITISH ARCHITECTS, JUNE 13TH, 1859.

I HAVE undertaken to render an account of the results of some studies of the Principles of Proportion in Architecture, as exemplified in the Parthenon.

The subject is not proposed as one of mere archæological interest, or simply as a curious chapter from the history of the art; if justice can be done to it, it ought to be something more—it ought to be a contribution to the scientific aids and resources of the art, as proving not merely that the Greeks worked upon such and such arbitrary maxims, but that they had discovered certain principles. To trace a theory of proportion as employed by the Greeks in design may be of interest in any case, but how much the more should it approve itself as having a rational and scientific basis.

Few here, it is probable, will doubt that the solution of one of these problems involves that of the other; and whoever can prove that he holds the explanation of the proportions of the Parthenon, will be easily absolved from further argument that the system employed was right and truly scientific; as, on the other hand, a claim to possess a true theory would have to stand the test of application to the Parthenon. The general theme of admiration of all who write and all who speak of the impression of this temple on the spectator, I have found to be the sense of harmony that it excites—the pleasurable satisfaction of the feelings associated with proportion; grace of proportion, dignity of proportion, justness and harmony of proportion, are phrases that recur in the course of their observations again and again. In response to what is implied in these expressions, the speculative have not been remiss in asserting for architectural harmony as close a dependence on mathematics as has been so long established for musical. Admitting the justness of the presumption so far, I may say at once that my own conclusions are quite at variance with what is often the next presumption, that the ratios of the diatonic scale have any special value as realised in architectural forms. I do not find this to be the case; I venture to say I find it distinctly not to be the case; but inasmuch as wherever numerous proportions are applied, on whatever principle, those which are found in the musical scale are sure to occur along with others, I can quite understand how the coincidences encourage a prepossessed or precipitate theorist, and flatter to betray.

It will be convenient to state succinctly in the first instance the most important conclusions, which will then be easily borne in mind through the process of proof and application.

First; it has appeared that the Greek architect attached the highest importance to the determination of his dimensions by proportion, and to the execution of those dimensions with minute exactness. Accidents and faults apart, for which a margin must be always allowed, nothing was left to chance, random, or remainder.

Secondly; dimensions are proportional, in the customary sense of the word, when they have a common measure; but it becomes of importance to decide in what directions they are most appropriately taken,—which lines are architecturally characteristic. I find that the Greek architects brought into comparison dimensions measured along the same straight lines, or lines parallel, and such a comparison for convenience I call Rectilinear proportion; thus the height of an entablature may be commensurable with the height of a column, the breadth of a metope with the breadth of a triglyph, the height of a naos door with the height of a pronaos column. Another important form of comparison is between dimensions taken at right angles to each other, and such instances will be referred to as Rectangular proportions. Thus it seems obvious and reasonable to estimate the proportion of an oblong plan by comparative statement of the length and breadth; no doubt its form might be recorded and communicated numerically by the statement of the angle of its diagonal with a side; but the eye does not judge such a proportion by reference to the diagonal.

The comparison of length and breadth of the temple measured upon the top step, of the height and length of an apartment, of the height and breadth of the façade, or a triglyph, &c., are examples of rectangular proportion.

The direct comparison of areas I only meet with in one, but that a very important class of instances; I refer to the determination of the relative proportion of columns by proportion of their sectional area, a subject which time forbids me to enter upon.

Assuming it to be determined that no dimension shall be admitted into a design that shall not be proportionate to some other dimension, either rectilinearly, rectangularly, or both ways, it still remains to be considered what proportions or what ratios (using an equivalent expression) shall be adopted. Ratios even of low numbers exclusively, offer themselves in crowds, and are to be subjected to arrangement and selection. If we commence with two equal lines, and, leaving one unaltered, alter the other by continuous diminutions, we shall find every conceivable or possible ratio occurring between absolute equality, 1 : 1 on the one hand, and absolute disparity, 1 : 0 on the other. If we pause at certain stages of the progress, as determined by some principle, these resting-places will form a scale of proportion, a series of steps by which we may regulate degree of approach to and departure from equality between any compared dimensions or series of dimensions. On what principles are the resting-places to be determined, the scales constructed? I can only give results briefly and partially too.

First; the design itself will necessitate the adoption of certain ratios from the requirements of purpose and plan.

Secondly; the variety of exigencies demand that the other selected ratios should range pretty widely over the interval to be divided, and give a choice of proportions verging towards inequality as well as towards equality, yet with sufficient interval to preclude confusing proximity.

Without pursuing the analysis further here, I must content myself with stating that the scale by which the Parthenon is regulated, commencing with the ratio 1 : 6, advances towards equality by ratios preserving the common difference between their terms of 5. Thus, 1 : 6, 2 : 7, 3 : 8, 4 : 9, 5 : 10, &c. As the scheme advances, the differences become trifling, and the numbers undesirably high, and the scale is made out by the ratios 4 : 5, 5 : 6, 6 : 7, &c., the common members of a primary series. Such a scale is formed by the rejection of the innumerable other ratios, some self-condemned by their high numbers, but others as not required or as interfering with the effect of the most characteristic ratios. Thus, the ratios 1 : 3 and 2 : 5, are most extensively and importantly employed in the temple at Bassæ, but are absolutely unknown in the Parthenon. Even of the members of the scale admissible and admitted some are comparatively neglected, while emphasis is given to a few by repetition in many instances, and both rectilinearly and rectangularly, and in applications expressive and important. Such predominance we shall find to be given in the Parthenon to the ratios 4 : 9, 7 : 12, and 9 : 14,—to the first especially. It is to be assumed that the system of making dimensions proportionate to each other, sometimes rectilinearly and sometimes rectangularly, was adopted on the principle that the mind and eye naturally take cognizance of both forms of comparison, and feel satisfaction in both harmonies. What then, it may be said, are their comparative values when they clash? It was the aim and study of the Greek architect of the Parthenon that they should not clash; and we shall have to admire the dexterity and success with which he harmonised the two forms of comparison, so that rectilinear proportions that fall out as happily as if they had been exclusively considered, are found to be compatible with, indeed to be the means of bringing about, rectangular comparisons that are still more effective; but I must leave it for the examples to bring home the value of this principle, and the skill evinced in employing it.

To the examples again I must trust for conveying due appreciation of the strict and logical consistency with which the Greek architect selected the terms of his comparisons; that the length of an apartment should be brought into proportion to its breadth, may be obvious enough, but in the ramification of design divisions are called for which must not be proportioned at random, but can only be correctly referred by a shrewd eye for correlative function and expression. Proportions, to be expressive, must correspond with and so represent natural relations of analogy or antithesis, and it was in the discernment or contrivance of these that Genius founded and perfected Greek architecture.

The terms to which a prerogative importance is allowed in regulating other dimensions are, especially,

      1. The breadth of the front, from which are derived,

      2. The breadth of the abacus, and

      3. The lower diameter of the column.

But no subdivision of these into any moderate number of fixed minutes or modules will explain their regulating power, which is dependent upon variable proportion, upon the adoption of ratios that may be taken from any part of the scale.

The designer of a Greek temple held it of importance to secure a definite proportion of low numbers between the length and breadth of the structure, as taken upon the grand stylobate, whether upon the topmost or on a lower step; a horizontal rectangular proportion. Thus the Parthenon has breadth and length on top step as 4 : 9, the Theseum the same, but on the lower step, and the temple at Bassæ also on lower step, has the proportion of 2 : 5, and the temple at Ægina that of a double square.

Equally important, or even more so, was it that the full vertical height of the front, from the pavement of the peribolus to the apex of the pediment, should compare in a ratio of low numbers. In several hexastyle temples, those of Theseus and Bassæ are examples, and, I may add, the western front of the Propylæa, the height of the front is commensurate with the breadth, as 3 : 4. In the Parthenon we shall find that, besides this grand ratio of height and breadth, which there is 9 : 14, very accurate rectangular proportions were obtained between other main divisions of the elevation; the check upon multiplying these in every instance, was the stringent importance of certain rectilinear proportions which were liable to interfere with them. Of these it appears, from comparison of examples, that the greatest importance was attached to making the height of the column exceed the joint height of the other members, that is, stylobate, entablature, and pediment, by a single aliquot. For example, the height of the column may compare with the complementary height of the front as 7 : 6, or as 6 : 5, &c., &c. In other words, the height of the column as compared with complement of height is the larger term in what is technically called a super-particular ratio. The ratio applied in the Parthenon is 10 : 9; in the Theseum 5 : 4, equivalent to 10 : 8. The Sicilian builders never discovered or appreciated this principle, and their effects suffer accordingly.

Thus much for the elevation of the front; but a farther arrangement was thought necessary or desirable in the Parthenon, in order to harmonise the column as vertical member with the joint horizontals, the entablature and stylobate, as seen on flank, where from such frequented points of view the height of the roof was not visible or brought into comparison. Accordingly the joint height of the stylobate and entablature on the flank is just equal to half the height of the column; or say, height of column : complement on flank :: 2 : 1. With what exactness this is the case will appear from the comparison of figures to be given presently. The same ratio holds good in the like comparison in the Theseum, where the entablature received an addition of height from the cymatium, which, as discovered by Mr. Penrose, was returned along its entire length.

It was a further established principle that the height of the column should compare symmetrically with the horizontal spacing of the columns; should, in fact, be just equal to the dimensions from the centre or edge of one column to the centre or edge of a third, measured upon the plan. In the Parthenon this symmetry is applied to three ordinary columns and the two intercolumns included, and the same appears to be the case at Sunium. In the east front of the Propylæa and in the temple at Bassæ an angle column and columniation are included in the comparison, which, in the latter case at least, introduces a difference from the relative contraction of the angle columniation. In the temple at Rhamnus the dimension is taken from the outer edge of the angle column to the centre of the third from the angle; in the Theseum we have a like division, but involving only ordinary columns.

I apprehend that the introduction of these equalities of heights with breadths was found to give repose to the effect of a long range of columns, as a repetition of similar spaces and dimensions, and the principle may be susceptible of wide application, as in fenestrated compositions. If in the progress of a design we conceive the diameter and spacing of the columns to be settled in the first instance, it is clear that the principle just stated would limit the architect to choice of height among three or four fixed dimensions, and, on the other hand, if the height of the column is assumed, the systems of spacing that are available would be reduced within narrow limits. In point of fact, in all such cases, no one point was settled absolutely until all others were settled. When the result is obtained it appears as if the adoption of one harmony brings about another as a necessary consequence; but this is not an accident, for the decision to adopt the first was made on the very ground that it was compatible with or involved a second; in all such adjustments the search is for those symmetries and proportions which recommend themselves by bringing the richest dower of subsidiary harmonies conducive to the effect required, and no solution is satisfactory until such are found.

One more principle, much taken to heart by the architects of the Doric temples of Greece proper, was to adopt a breadth for the abacus of the capital equal to $\frac{1}{5}$ of the height of the column, or else an aliquot part of the breadth of the temple on the top step, or, lastly, accommodating both conditions. A dimension for this part, however, cannot be adopted lightly, for it decides the diameter of the echinus at its greatest swell, and this must be relative to the general proportions required for the column. At Bassæ the abacus of the front is $\frac{1}{5}$ of the height of the column, but not commensurable with the top step; in the Theseum it is $\frac{1}{5}$ of the height of the column, and also $\frac{1}{12}$ of the top step; in the Parthenon the ordinary abacus of the east front is $\frac{1}{15}$ of the top step, but not commensurable with the height of the column; the abacus of an angle column, however, which is broader than the ordinary, is equal in breadth to $\frac{1}{5}$ of the height of the column, while on the other hand it is, of course, no aliquot of the top step.

Such were the leading conditions to which by custom of the style, by experience of good effect, or by manifest fitness, the architect's design was bound to conform, which gave a certain guidance at the same time that they gave a certain control; not so much guidance that responsibility for ultimate effect did not rest with his genius, not so much control that genius had not ample range for variety and invention.

We have now therefore, in the case of the Parthenon, a clear breadth of front of 100 Attic feet, say 101·341, on which to erect an octastyle Doric portico, with diameters of columns proportioned to intercolumns in about the ratio 4 : 5; and in the distribution of the eight columns we have to take into account that, in accordance with the style, the angle columns are to have a somewhat larger diameter, and the angle intercolumns are to be somewhat more contracted than the rest. The process by which, it appears to me, the architect made the distribution in the present instance, is as follows:—The top step had to be divided into seven main segments, five of them being equal, and giving the lines of centres for six columns equidistant from each other, while the two end segments were to be somewhat larger, in order to receive the full diameters of the angle columns—a difference that more than makes up for the contraction of the angle intercolumniation. The problem therefore, in the first instance, is to assign the degree of excess to the two angle segments, as the breadth of the front divided by seven, after deduction of this joint excess, would give columniation. The seven segments of the step correspond to seven segments of the architrave, each equal, in a general way, to the breadth of two triglyphs and two metopes, except the external segments, which have to accommodate an additional half triglyph. Now, if we deduct the breadth of a semi-triglyph from each end of the step, and divide the intermediate space by seven, we shall find the divisions give us the ordinary columniations with the greatest accuracy. This process, of course, assumes that we know the breadth of the triglyph, and this may easily have been obtained before the average columniation was absolutely settled, as it is deducible proportionably from the breadth of the architrave.

	Triglyph.		Columniation.		Ang. Seg.		Measured.
101·341 −	2·786 =	98·555 ÷	7 = 14·079 + 1·393 = 15·472	Cf.	15·478, 15·367,
228·141 −	,, =	225·355 ÷	16 = 14·084 + ,, = 15·477		15·468, 15·449, 15·531, 15·443.

We have now therefore obtained the centres of the columns, giving columniation 14·084, which is exactly coincident with a great many as measured, and also with the average of the variations, the principle of which is accurately determinable, but cannot be now discussed. If we divide this calculated columniation into nine parts, and assign four to the diameter and five to the intercolumn, we obtain, $14·084 \div 9 = 1·565 \times 5 = 7·825$, intercolumn; $14·084 \div 9 = 1·565 \times 4 = 6·260$, diameter. The measured diameters give 6·250 and even 6·245, and this may be held a sufficient approximation; still I believe that another principle decided the exact dimension adopted, though the difference may be but little more than the ⅛ of an inch. Again we are entitled, by the usage of the order, to look out for an agreement between the height of the column and a division of the colonnade on plan. The nearest approximation is given by the dimension on plan that includes three diameters and two ordinary intercolumns, viz., 34·428, but the height of the column is only 34·250, giving a difference of full two inches. Here again, while we are bound to admit that this approximate symmetry was regarded and valued, it is clear that we cannot accept it as governing the dimensions adopted in execution for the height of columns.

I will first go over the scheme of proportions by which I conceive this and the other divisions of the elevation to have been decided, and afterwards give the comparative tabulation of the dimensions as they come out by calculation, and as set down in the monumental survey of the temple made by Mr. Penrose for the Society of Dilettanti, and published by them in 1851.

The proportion of the height of the front to the breadth of the top step is as 9 : 14. The breadth of the front is to the length of the temple as 4 : 9, as we have seen; and it is a necessary consequence of these proportions that the height of the front should compare with the length of the temple as 2 : 7. These therefore are the grand circumscribing proportions of the structure; the only inaccuracy is that the measured height of the front is ½ an inch higher than it should be by calculation; but the actual length of the temple compares with the height thus enhanced in the ratio 2 : 7, with absolute exactness within $\frac{4}{1000}$ of a foot.

$$2 : 65\cdot185 : : 7 : 228\cdot147 \text{ Cf. measured } 228\cdot141.$$

It will be observed that the ratios, 2 : 7, 4 : 9, and 9 : 14, have respectively the common difference between their terms, of 5. In the recited order the terms approach towards equality, and the series may be extended by insertion of intermediate and other ratios having the same characteristic, thus—

$$1 : 6, \ 2 : 7, \ 3 : 8, \ 4 : 9, \ 5 : 10, \ \&c.$$

It will be found that several of these ratios are repeated with marked intention in the Parthenon, while none whatever are employed in the design that do not belong to the series either directly or as equivalents (as 2 : 3 = 10 : 15, &c.). The height of the front thus obtained is divided between height of column and of complement, in the ratio 10 : 9, which gives 34·288 for the column, to compare with 34·250, the measured height of the angle column. From the complementary height we have now to deduct a dimension equal to half the height of the column, viz., 17·125, to be distributed between the stylobate and the entablature, so that the height of the column shall be just ⅔ of the height from the level of the peribolus to the base of the antefixal ornaments on flank. The remainder of the complementary height belongs to the pediment, and proves just equal to the breadth of the ordinary columination.

It will be observed, that it still remains to complete the horizontal division of the front by apportionment of dimension between entablature and stylobate. The axioms of proportional design as conceived by the Greeks require here that the rectilinear proportion adopted shall also bring about or be consistent with a certain number of very important rectangular proportions. On general considerations it may be easily determined to give a larger share of the dimension at command to the entablature;

but the question still remains, how much more? How much more precisely, and why? In effect the apportionment was made by giving 6 parts in height to the stylobate as against 11 to the entablature; the ratio 6 : 11, it will be observed, belongs to the series already specified.

The rectangular proportions conciliated by such division are these:—The joint height of column and entablature comes out exactly commensurable with the hundred Attic feet in the breadth of front in the ratio 4 : 9, which is the proportion of the plan; consequently, as the length of the top step is to its breadth, so is that breadth to the joint height of column and entablature.

Again, by the dimensions assigned by calculation, the breadth of the top step is commensurable with the joint height of column, entablature, and pediment as 12 : 7 nearly; by the addition,—by the adjusting increment, of half an inch to the pediment, the comparison becomes exact, with the further advantage of making the height of the pediment equal to one columniation.

Let us now compare the tabulated dimensions as furnished by Mr. Penrose's independent and scrupulous measurements, which are accessible to all, and as deducible by the process I have set forth:—

```
                    Calculated.                                              Measured.
14 :: 9 : 101·341 : 65·1478 full height of front ..................... 65·185
 9 :: 10 :  30·859 : 34·288 height of angle column ................. 34·253
10 ::  9 :  34·288 : 30·859 complement of front.................... 30·932
                    ─────
                    65·147 full height as calculated above............65·185

       Ht. of Column.
 2 :: 1 : 34·288 : 17·144 stylobate + entablature ................ 17·150 on flank.
11 :: 6 : 11·093 :  6·050 height of stylobate ......................  6·058
 6 :: 11 :  6·050 : 11·093 entablature on flank.................. ⎫
                    ─────   i.e. + returned fillet of cymatium ......... ⎬ 11·092
                    17·143 joint stylobate and entablature as above.    ⎭

From calculated height of front ..................... 65·147
Deduct calculated entablature ............ 11·093
    "        "       column   ............ 34·288
    "        "       stylobate............  6·050   51·431
                                                   ─────
Remainder for pediment ........................ 13·716
Add height of fillet of cymatium only present in ⎫
    entablature on flank......................... ⎭  0·299
Add increment, as referred to above ................:  0·037·
                                                   ─────
                          14·052 height of pediment 14·073
```

Entablature on front, calculated.......................... 10·794
Column, calculated .... 34·288

Height from pavement to apex, calculated............. 59·134 ⎫
                                                                              ⎬
12 :: 7 : 101·341 : .... 59·115 ⎭ Cf. measured ... 59·127
9 :: 4 : 101·341 : 45·0426 column + entablature on front...... do. 42·046

With respect to the vertical division of the entablature, the frieze and architrave are made equal within a minute difference, which is given in favour of the architrave, and scarcely amounts to $\frac{1}{8}$ of an inch. The thickness of the horizontal cornice on front is derived from the height of the frieze by the ratio 4 : 9. It is therefore easy to divide the height of the entablature by 22, and assign 4 parts to cornice and 9 each to architrave and frieze.

9 :: 4 : Frieze 4·417 : 1·963 Cf. measured 1·951.

The perpendicular thickness of the raking cornice with its cymatium, at the apex of the pediment, is derived from the horizontal cornice, to which it is proportioned as 4 : 3.

I may add here, that the height of the capital is derived from the diameter of the angle column by the ratio 4 : 9, viz., 9 : 4 :: 6·378 : 2·834 to compare with measured 2·833. Again, the breadth of the triglyph is derived by the same ratio from the lower diameter of the ordinary column, viz., 9 : 4 :: 6·250 : 2·777. Compare measured 2·766.

The height of the stylobate is determined by the proportions of the elevation, but it still remains to assign a projection for its lowest step. The actual projection that is the joint breadth of the lower steps, is 4·997, which brings the following relations into harmony :—

6 : 5 :: 6·058 height of stylobate : 5·048 projection (4·997).

5 : 4 :: diam. of ordinary col. 6·250 : 5·00 (measured 4·997).

Thus, the intercolumn is to diameter as diameter is to projection of steps.

We cannot too highly appreciate the force and vigour that the composition gains by the feeling with which the artist has tempered the horizontality of the steps by the predominance of verticality in their profile. It is by the thickness of the stylobate exceeding its projection in the ratio of 6 : 5, while that of the column falls below the breadth of its correlative, the intercolumn, in the ratio 4 : 5, that it acquires an expression of superior solidity corresponding to its function of bearing the columns, though in reality of smaller dimension than a diameter. The effect is assisted and enhanced by the steepness of the top step, the proper stylobate, as compared with those below. The height assigned to it seems to have been derived from the diameter of the angle column by the normal ratio 2 : 7, viz. :—

7 : 2 :: 6·378 diam. of angle col. : 1·822 height of top step (1·814 measured).

We must now proceed to an abstract of the considerations of proportion which seem to have governed the distribution of the plan between peristyle, cella, and divisions of cella. The primary concern is to determine the line of the upper step, or proper basement of the cella, relatively to the parallel line of the upper step of the grand peristyle. The anta is placed at such a distance from the edge of the stylobate, that the sum of its breadth and the interval between it and a flank column exactly equals a columniation. To state this differently, the dimension, including diameter of column on flank of anta and interval between them, exactly equals the sum of the diameters of two adjacent columns on flank and the interval between them; and inasmuch as the anta is less in diameter than a column, the difference goes to enhance the interval or void. The process of division is, therefore, the simplest conceivable. Set off on the front from angle of top step a dimension equal to an ordinary columniation plus an ordinary diameter, say 20·34; this gives the lateral distance for the inner angle of the anta; assign a breadth to the anta which has a ratio to the diameter of column as 4 : 5, and this gives the outer angle of the anta, and the line of the cella step on flank.

The next, and a most important consideration, is the extent of the top step of the cella east and west—its distance from the parallel line of stylobate on either front. Here we find that by continued gradation, the interval between step of cella and edge of top step of grand stylobate is made greater on front than on flank, exceeds it in fact at the east front in the ratio of 8 : 7, being the exact ratio in which the interval from cella wall to flank column exceeds the intercolumn.

8 : 7 :: 17·138 : 14·997..................... (measured 15·00.)
8 : 7 :: 8·920 : 7·805..................... (measured 7·818, &c.)

The artist, however, who decided these proportions had regard at the same time to their compatibility with some others that are of the highest importance; the cella, which was to be distributed among apartments that were required to have definite proportions, could not have its length relatively to its breadth determined at random. Measured on the top step it has very exactly a ratio of breadth to length as 7 : 19; thus, 7 : 19 :: 71·33 : 193·61, which varies from measured length 193·733 on flank by deficiency of ·123, and this difference seems to be but the reappearance of the error 0·125 that we have noticed in length of the grand stylobate from just ratio to its breadth. The ratio 7 : 19 seems at first sight unhandsome and undesirable, from the high number it includes, and the great difference between its terms; indeed, had the architect made the lower step of the cella longer by 0·68, it would have had the admissible proportion of 3 : 8, the change, however, involving a sacrifice of graces which he did not allow himself to be tempted to make. His justification and purpose become readily apparent. If we deduct an exact square from an oblong 7 : 19, we are manifestly left with an oblong reduced to the ratio 7 : 12, and this is the division which has been adopted. The breadth of the cella 71·33 is just equal to the dimension from the top step of the posticum to the back of the opisthodomus, including the thickness of the transverse wall of partition (71·334), and consequently the same breadth compared with the remainder of length, the dimension from the transverse wall in the naos to the edge of the pronaos step, necessarily bears to it the ratio 7 : 12, the same ratio that occupies so important a place in the elevation of the façade.

I believe it to have been in order to help the value of this proportion, that the pavements of the naos and pronaos were made almost exactly upon a level, and thus, when the portal was thrown open, the spectator might easily take both dimensions together within the scope of vision.

From the stringency of the general proportions applied in the opisthodomus it is clear that we must expect at least equal care in the more important naos; it is also clear that, whatever difficulties may have occurred in distributing the naos, they were overcome not by sacrificing the proportions of the opisthodomus but by effectually reconciling them. But by this distribution the plan of the proper opisthodomus itself is brought out with depth and breadth very accurately proportioned, as 11 : 16. The clear interior breadth, on level of the pavement, is 62·570 (viz., 4·380 × 2 = 8·760 + 62·570 = 71·330), and the corresponding depth, as shown on plan, is 43·003. Now, 16 : 11 :: 62·570 : 43·016, a result which may be considered absolutely identical.

The uncertainty that exists, from the condition of the ruins, as to the height originally assigned by the architect to the interior of the naos and of the opisthodomus, hampers our investigation of the considerations by which he decided the distribution of the plan.

I have shown that the architect divided the platform of his cella by a transverse line, which gave an exact square for partition wall, opisthodomus, and posticum, and an oblong of the proportion 7 : 12 for the naos and pronaos. Assuming the thickness of the flank walls to be determined, the clear interior breadth of the apartments is given, and it remains to place the walls of the door jambs, on either front, at such distances from the wall of partition as to afford plans for the apartments of desirable proportions, and also leave fitting remainders for pronaos and posticum. Accordingly, the pronaos wall is so placed as to make the length of the naos 98·095, which compares with the sheer breadth from wall to wall of 63·01, in ratio 14 : 9. That is to say, the ichnography of the grand apartment,—of the naos, has precisely the same ratio between its dimensions, taken rectangularly, that obtains between the breadth of the temple and its full height on front from pavement of peribolus to apex of pediment.

14 : 9 :: 98·095 : 63·06 (measured 63·01).

This is the third example of a repetition of a special rectangular proportion, on plan and on elevation, and in positions corresponding in relative importance; the others being 7 : 12, and 4 : 9. The thickness given to the pronaos wall equals the breadth of an abacus, and it happily results that the dimensions from the pronaos wall to the line of lowest step on front is exactly double that from the edge of cella step to the same line of the stylobate returned on flank.

It seems to have been a traditional principle that the hecatompedon, or 100 feet, which, as we have seen, measures the breadth of the temple, should also apply to some manifest dimension of the naos. To the naos specifically the title Hecatompedæan is found ascribed in inscriptions, and we need not look far to find a coincidence as near as the nature of the case would require. The dimension from the back wall of the naos to the centre line of the threshold measures 101·470, to compare with the exact estimate of 101·341; and here the difference of 0·125 − 9 interferes a third time, and is finally disposed of.

I have now reached or rather exceeded the limits allowable for a paper. I am bound to observe that it is due to these limits that I have only been able to exemplify the theory by a selection of instances, and that there is not one application of proportion adduced that I cannot support by conclusive parallels in other Greek works. Although it is only in the Parthenon that all the refinements of the system are employed in all their perfection, yet each appears elsewhere separately, and so distinctly as to leave no doubt as to its recognition. These corroborations, therefore, I have been obliged to pretermit, for the same reason that I have avoided discussing rival systems, and the examination of the extent to which they involve truth, and the points at which, as it seems to me, fallacy supervenes.

Since the last paragraph above was written and read, an opportunity has been afforded me of putting forth illustrations of the Greek theory of architectural proportion as applied in other cases. They will be found in my Essay, admitted by Mr. Cockerell as an appendix to his magnificent work upon the temples at Bassæ and Ægina. Other examples are under my hand, worked out in equal detail from the materials found so fully in the publications of the Dilettanti Society. The flexibility and practical character, as well as the specific fitness of the system, can only be appreciated after observation of its success in varied application and numerous examples.

It has now become possible, and is a good work to be done by one who will face labour and some other contingencies, to republish all the best records of classical architecture, with measurements made available for proportional comparison by being expressed decimally, and with a well-studied exposition of the organic law of proportion pervading each composition. The designer of classical architecture—to speak of no other style—will never, until this is done by others or himself, feel or indeed be even comparatively safe out of sight of a precedent, and collections of works of genius will have no more noble fate than to be resorted to as pattern-books. Can the continuance of such an abuse be a necessity? The civilisation of the world and the arts that pertain to it were saved by bold resumption of research at the point where the ancient Greek had flagged or been forcibly interrupted; but the genius of the artists of the Revival did less for architecture than for any of the other arts, not excepting sculpture; and the greatest hope of all went down when Rafael, just as he had declared his dream of an ideal, and recognising both the aids and shortcomings of Vitruvius, was applying to the evolution of it, sickened and died. As some compensation, modern architectural students have at least the great advantage of purer Greek models as subjects for study, and suggestions of research. Hints are not wanting also, that the time is now again full ripe for a renewed effort to roll away an opprobrium inveterate for thousands of years. Signs are abroad of one of those great revulsions of opinion with which taste is ever sympathetic, which periodically cancel for ever, for all purposes of active mischief, the systematised mistakes of long generations; when this arrives to relieve the world, though it may not be to-day nor to-morrow, no doubt it will bring the refreshment with it of a regeneration of that art which by its nature is ever before us and about us, to plague or to delight, which in its worst phase has all the obtrusiveness of vulgarity, but in its better partakes of the condescension of the Divine.

BRADBURY AND EVANS, PRINTERS, WHITEFRIARS.

Fig. 4.

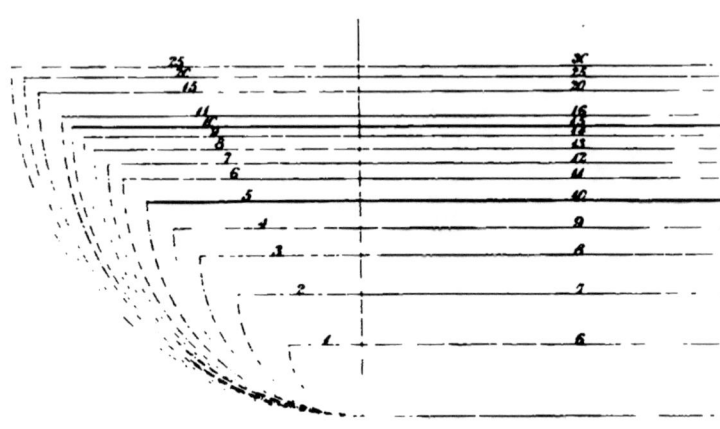

Scale of progressive Ratios having common difference between terms, of 5; in Rectilinear and also Rectangular arrangement

Fig. 5.

Proportional Scale of the Parthenon.

Fig. 1.

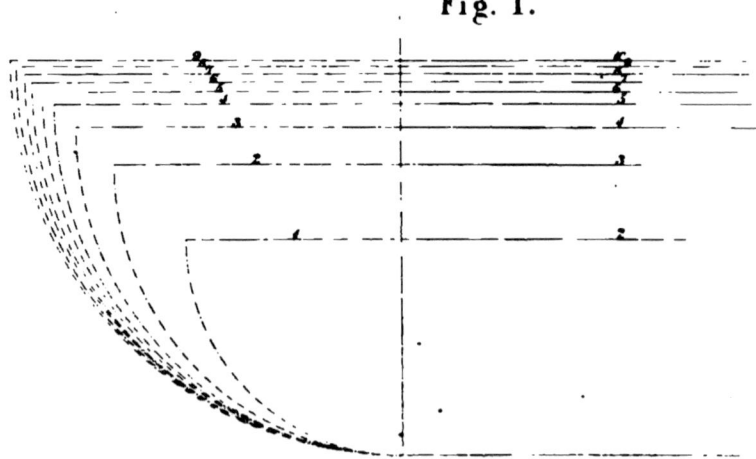

Scale of progressive Ratios having common difference between terms, of Unity; in Rectilinear and also Rectangular arrangement

PROPORTIO

W. W. Lloyd invent.

Plate 1.

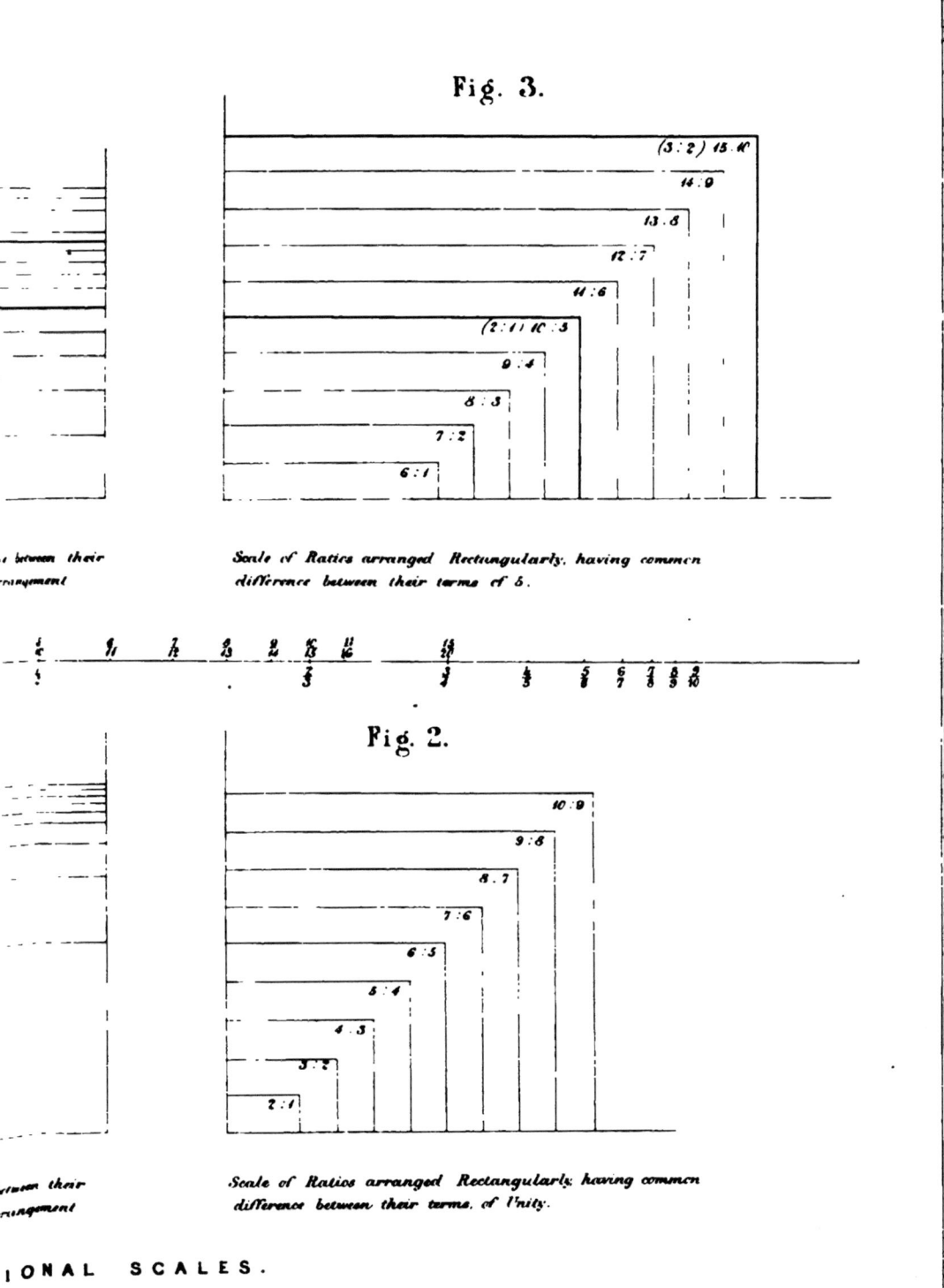

Fig. 3.

Scale of Ratios arranged Rectangularly, having common difference between their terms of 5.

Fig. 2.

Scale of Ratios arranged Rectangularly, having common difference between their terms, of Unity.

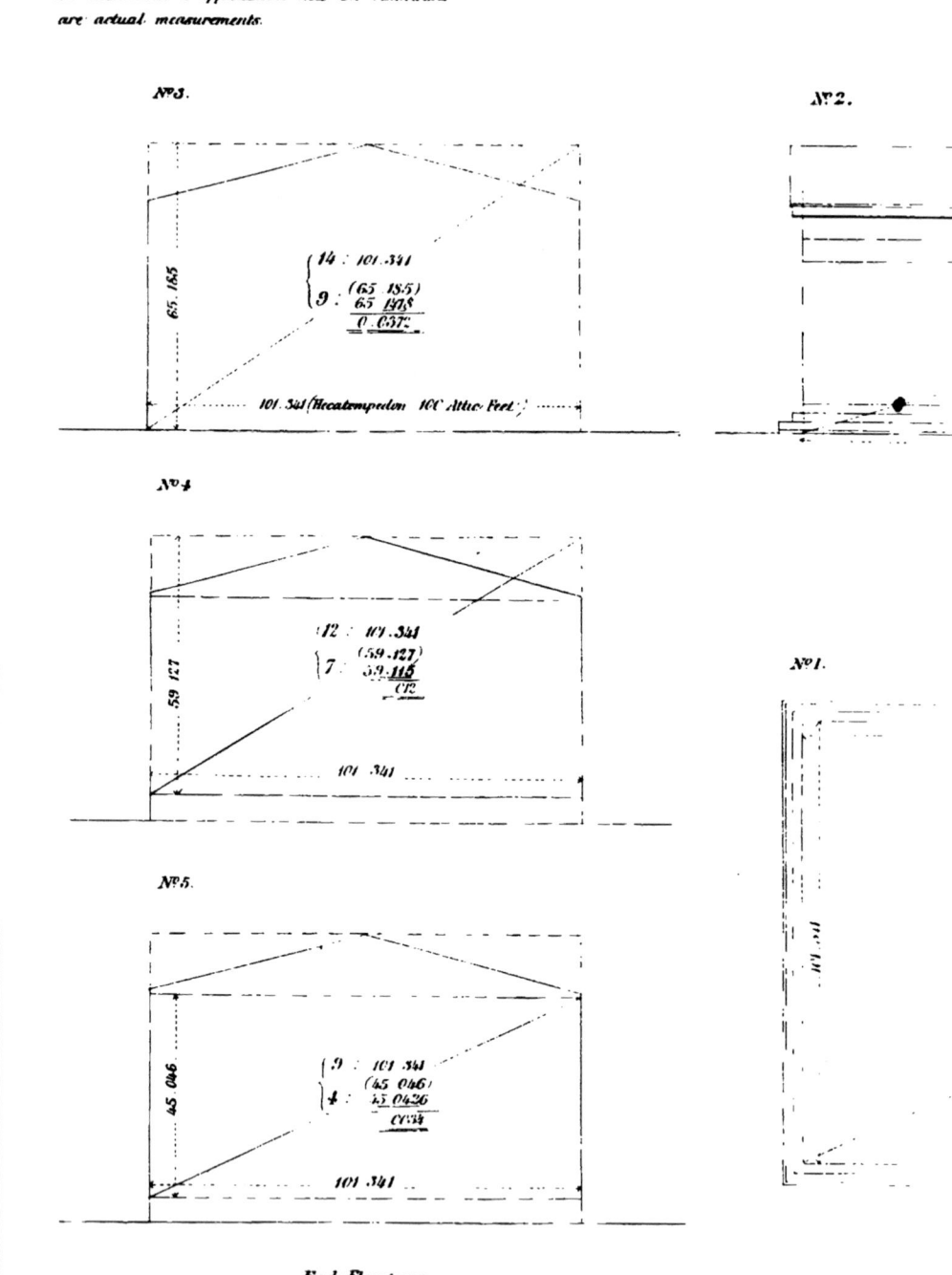

Plate 2.

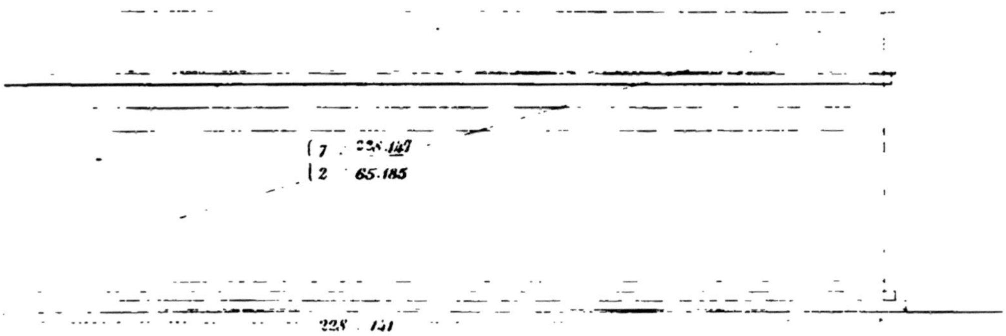

{7 – 228.447
{2 – 65.185

228.141

Side Elevation

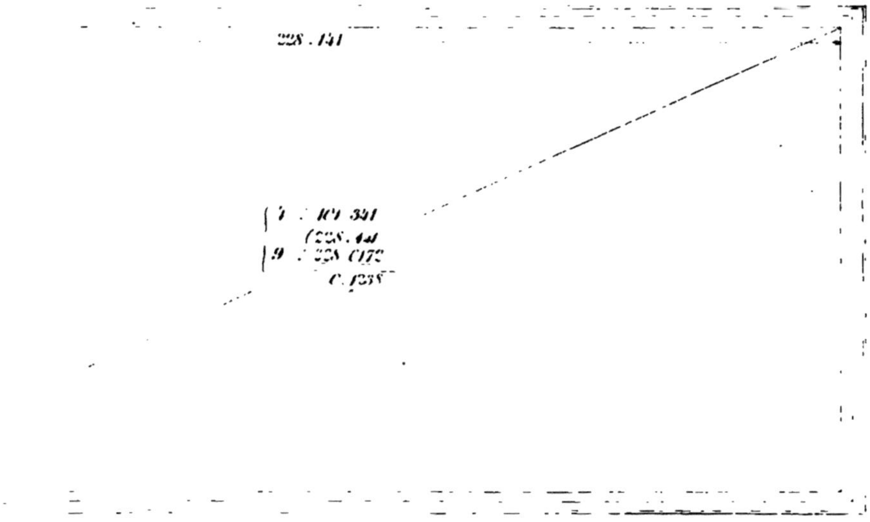

228.141

{7 – 101.341
{228.441
{9 – 228.0172
C. 1238

Plan

PARTHENON.

difference between their terms of 5
Elevation

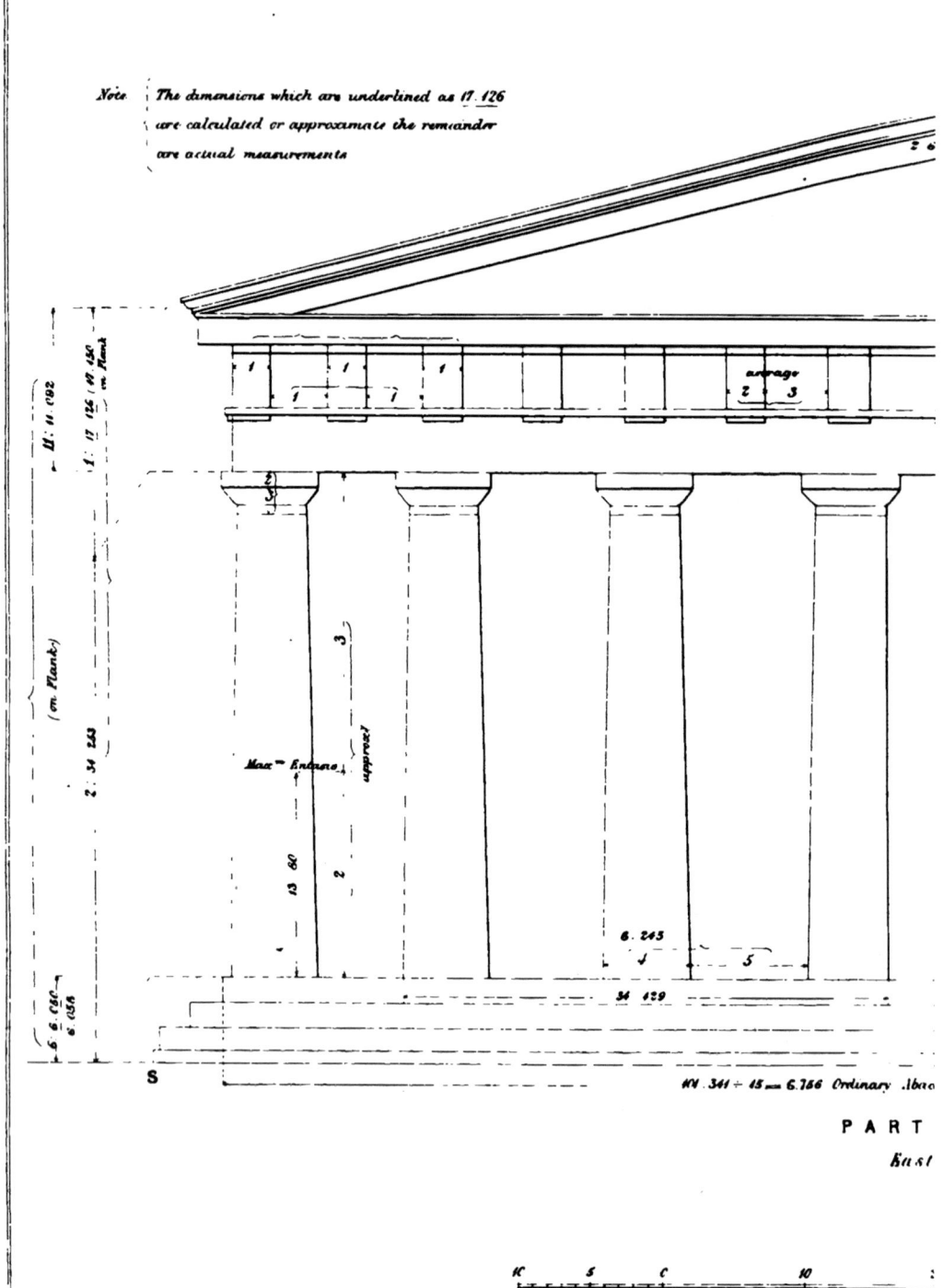

W.W. Lloyd, inven.

Plate 3.

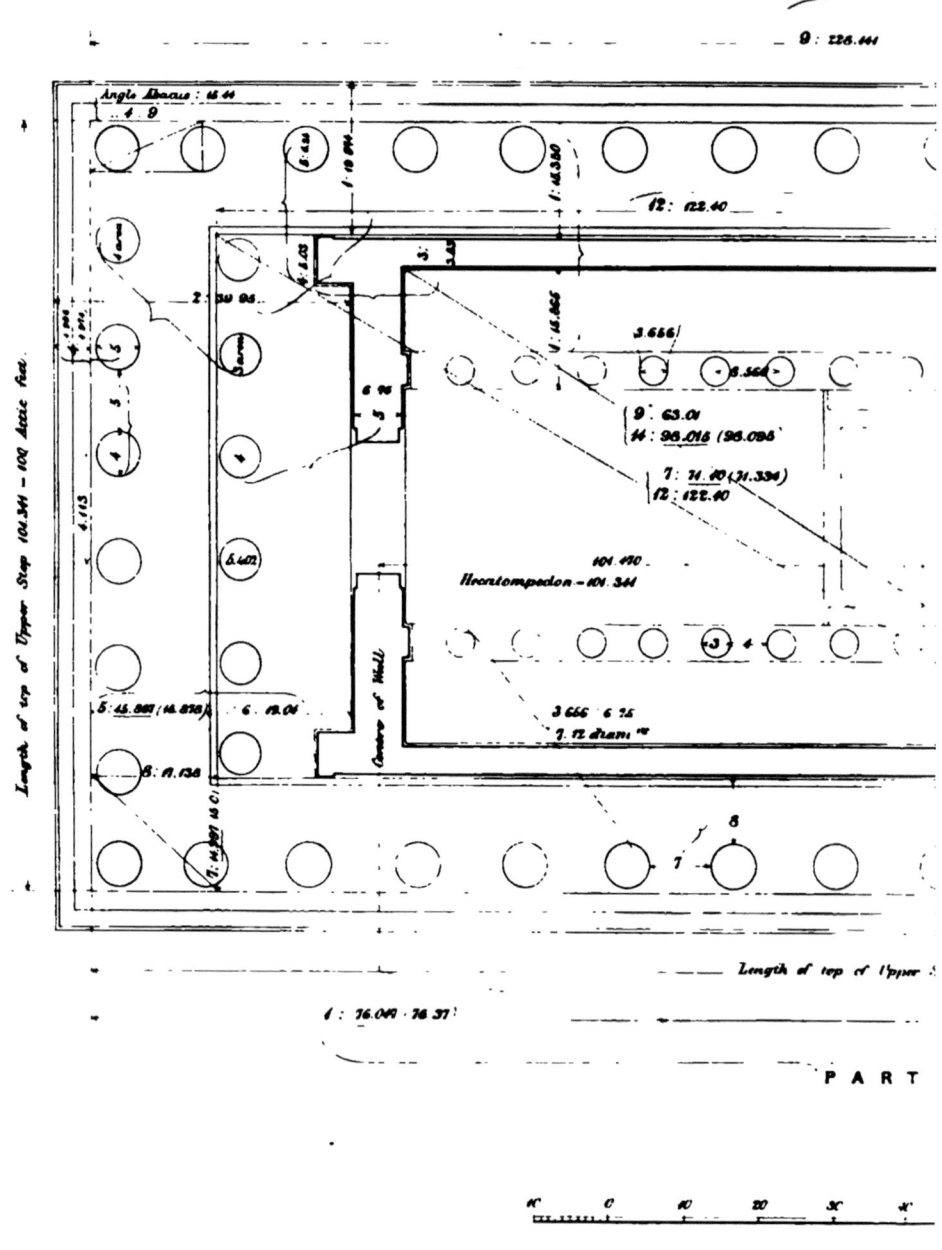

Plate 5.

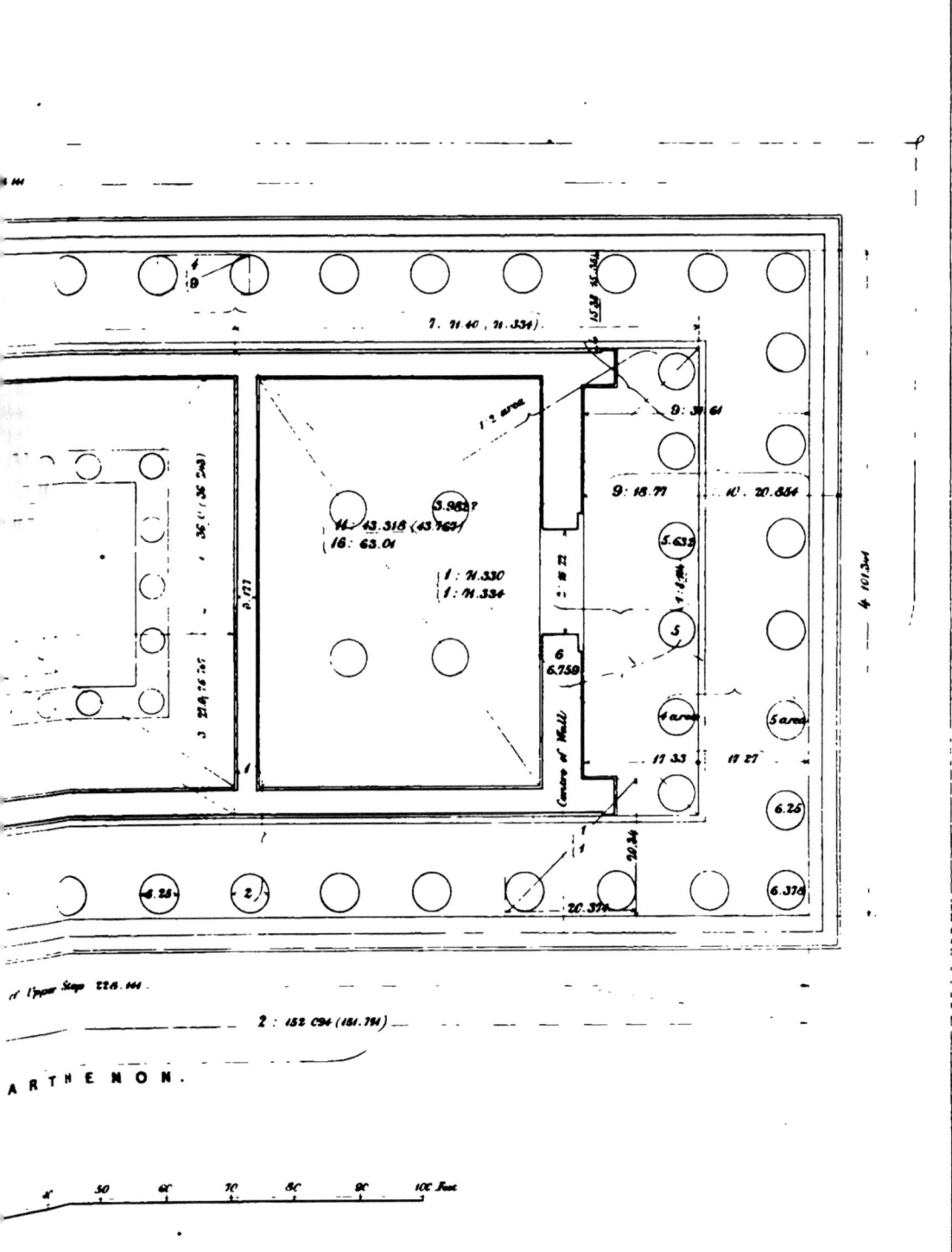

Plate 6

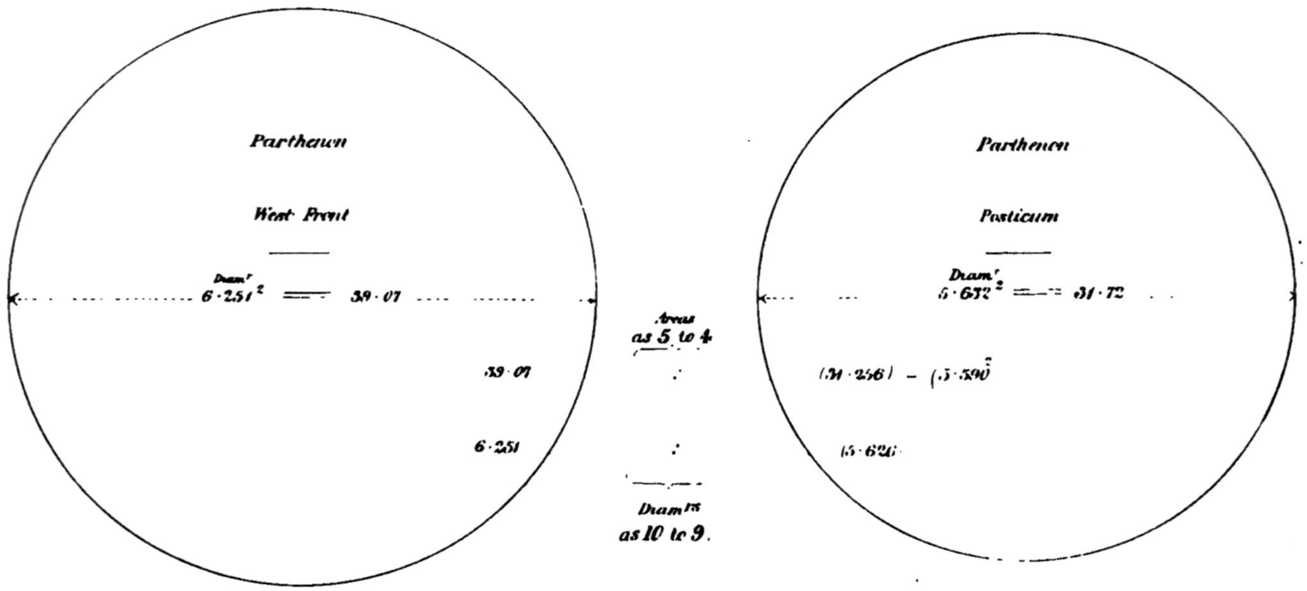

Parthenon

West Front

$\text{Diam}^r\ 6\cdot 251^2 = 39\cdot 07$

$39\cdot 07$

$6\cdot 251$

Areas as 5 to 4

Diam^rs as 10 to 9

Parthenon

Posticum

$\text{Diam}^r\ 5\cdot 652^2 = 31\cdot 72$

$(31\cdot 256) - (5\cdot 580^2)$

$(5\cdot 624)$

Note. The Dimensions within brackets are Calculated or approximate

Note. The dimensions within brackets are calculated or approximate.

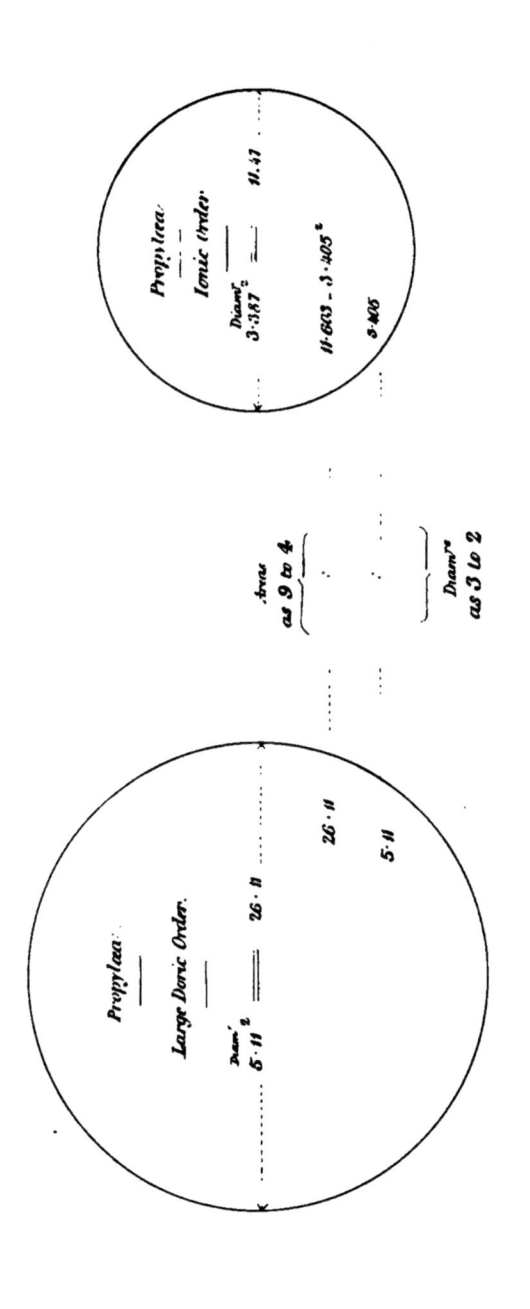

Propylæa
Ionic Order
Diam^r $\frac{}{3\cdot387}$ = 11.47
11·603 - 3·405^a
5·405

Propylæa
Large Doric Order
Diam^r $\frac{}{5\cdot11}$ = 26·11
26·11
5·11

Area as 9 to 4

Diam^r as 3 to 2

PARTHENON & PROPYLÆA.
(COLUMNS.)

W.W. Lloyd, invenᵗ.

Plate 7.

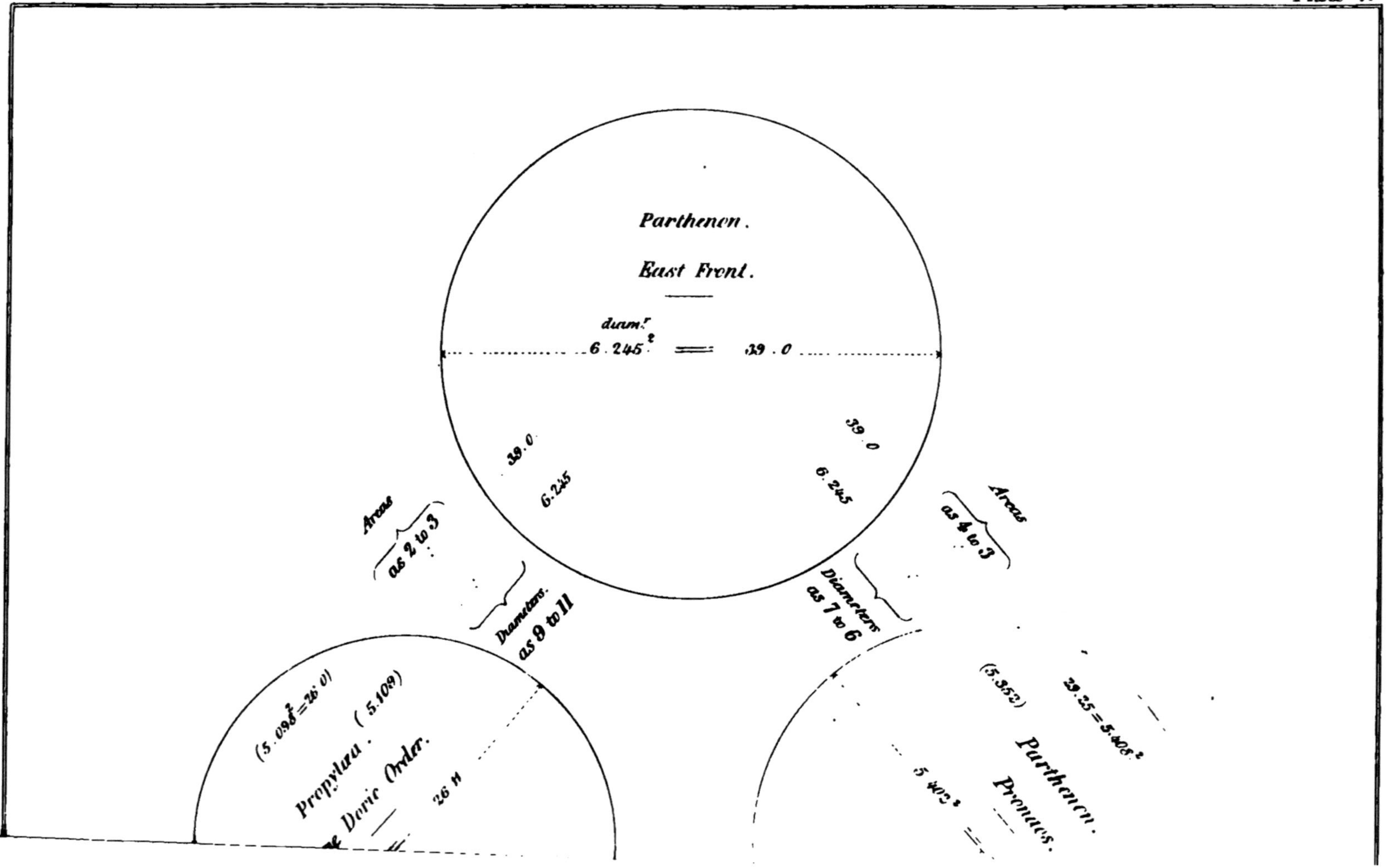

Parthenon.
East Front.
diamʳ
6.245
39.0
6.245
39.0
6.245
39.0

Areas
as 4 to 3

Diameters
as 7 to 6

39.25 = 5.408²
(5.352)
Parthenon.
Pronaos.
5.402²

Areas
as 2 to 3

Diameters
as 8 to 11

Propylæa.
Doric Order.
26.11
(5.109)
(5.098² = 26.0)

Parthenon.
Pronaos.
(5.402)² =
29.18
29.18
5.402

Areas
as 9 to 4

Diameters
as 3 to 2

12.97 = 3.601.²
(3.601)
Diam.²
3.656² = 13.36
Parthenon.
Naos.

Naos Diam.ʳ
(3.643)
3.656.

Peristyle Diam.ʳ
6.245
is to
as 12 to 7

Note. The Dimensions between brackets are the calculated or approximate.

Propylæa
Large Doric Order.
5.11² = 26.11
26.11
5.11

Diameters
as 11 to 6

Areas
as 1 to 2

Propylæa.
Small Doric Order.
3.516² = 12.36
(3.515)
(3.643² = 13.055)

PARTHENON & PROPYLÆA.
COLUMNS.

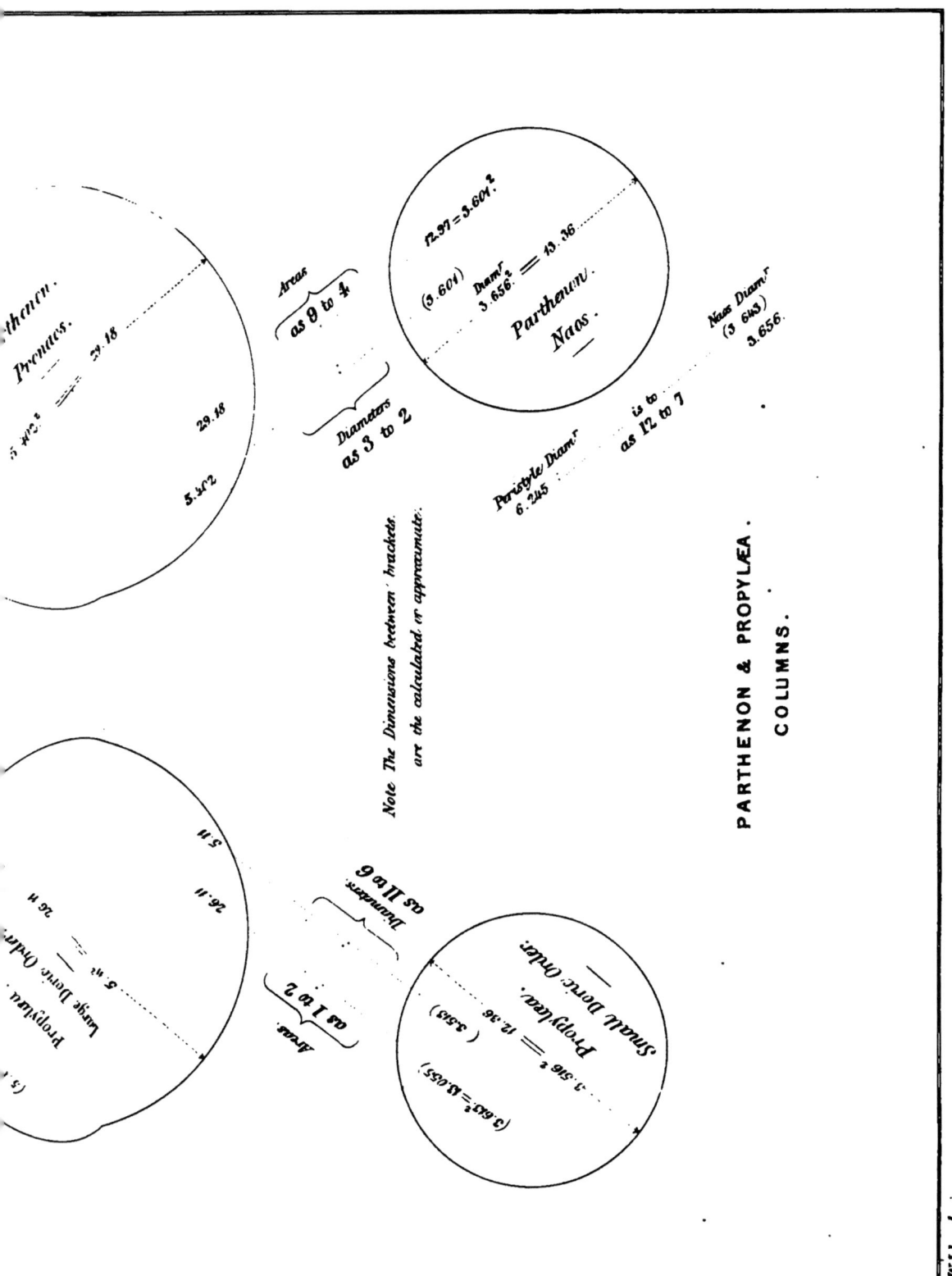

W. W. Lloyd, inven.

Plate 8.

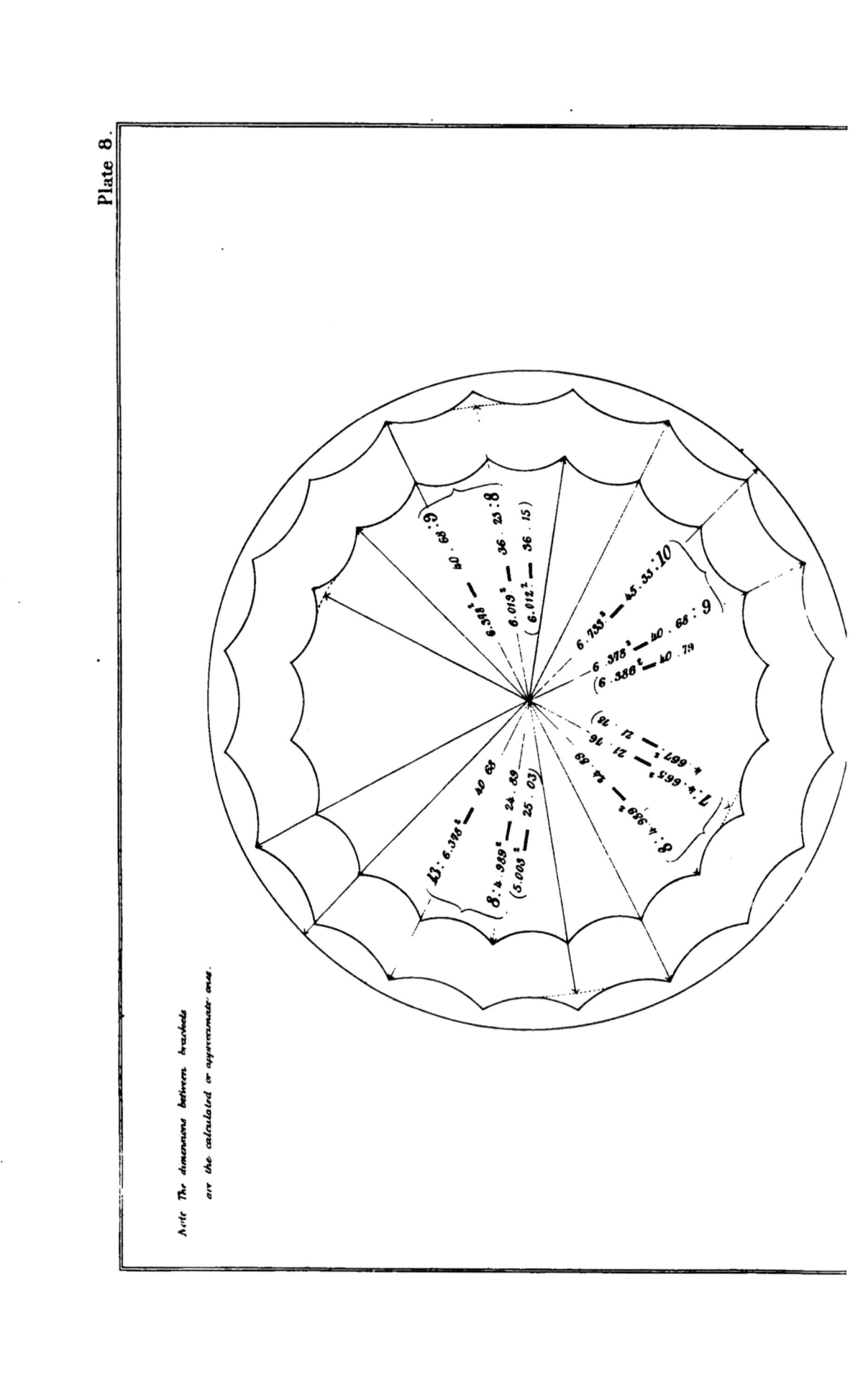

*Note. The dimensions between brackets
are the calculated or approximate ones.*

PARTHENON. S.E. ANGLE. COLUMN.

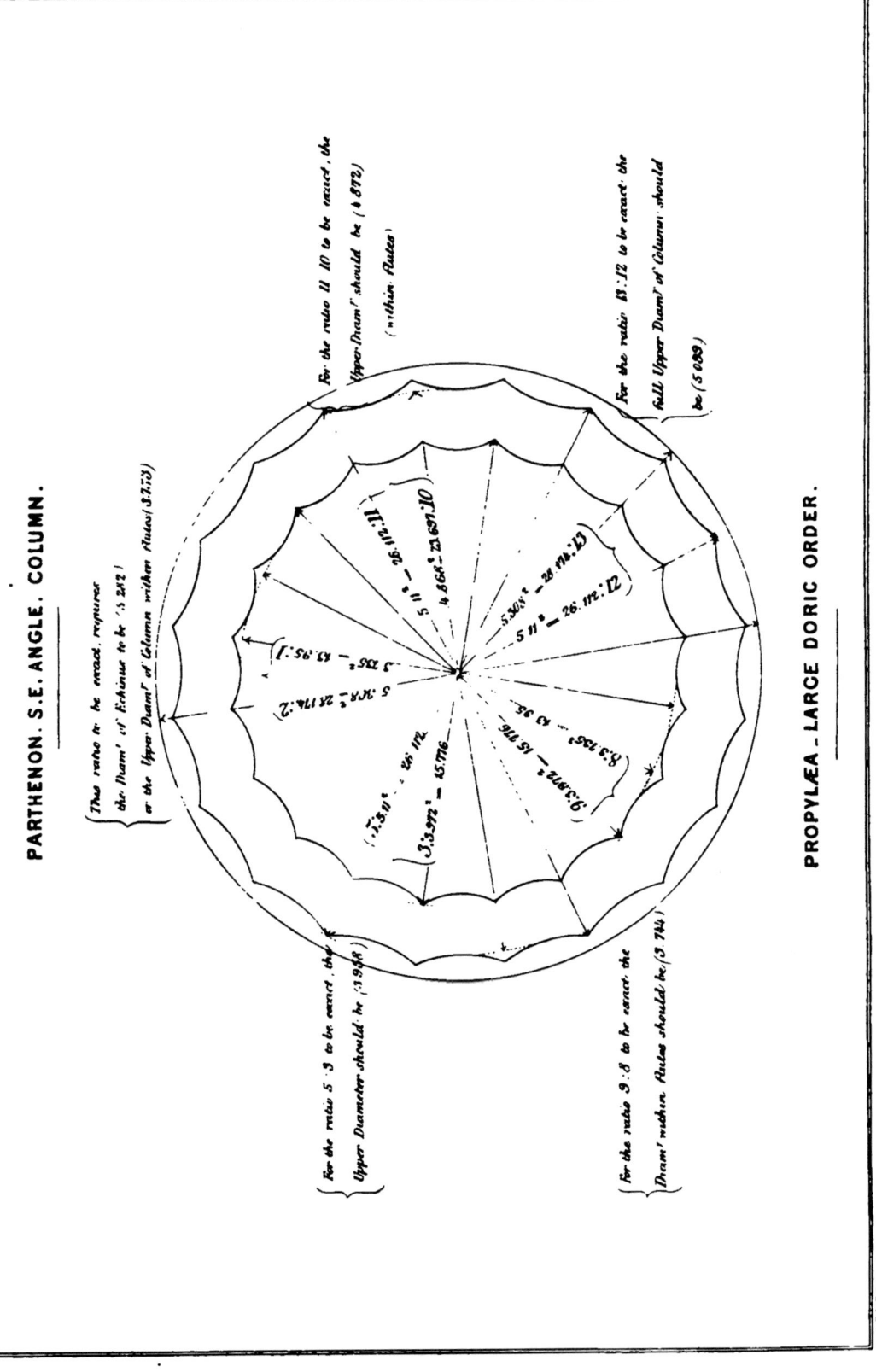

PROPYLÆA — LARGE DORIC ORDER.

W. W. Lloyd, inven.

Note. The dimensions which are underlined as 43.57, are the calculated or approximate ones, the remainder are measured.

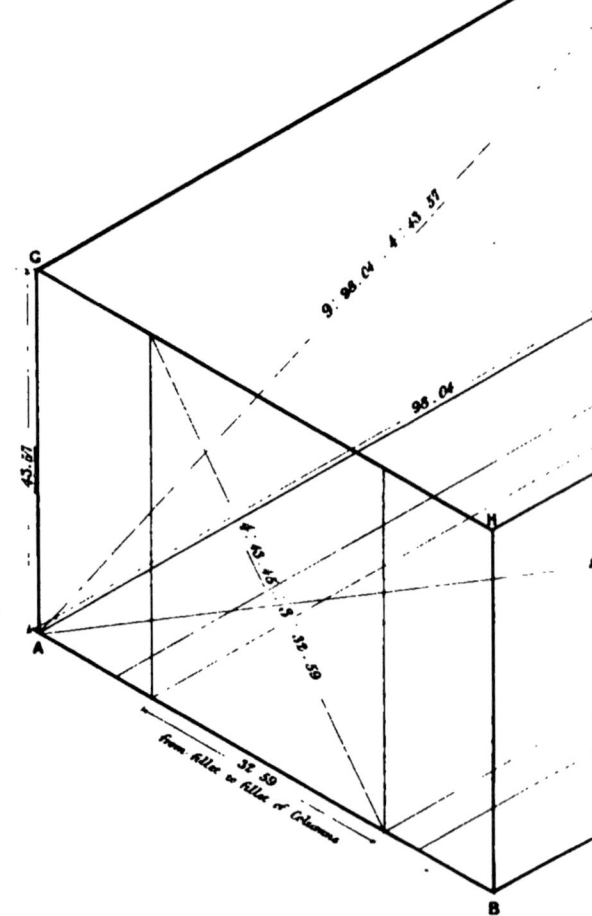

Note. The height given to the Naos (43.57) is conjectural.

OUTLINE OF THE NA
IN ISOMETRIC

W. W. Lloyd, inven.

Plate 9.

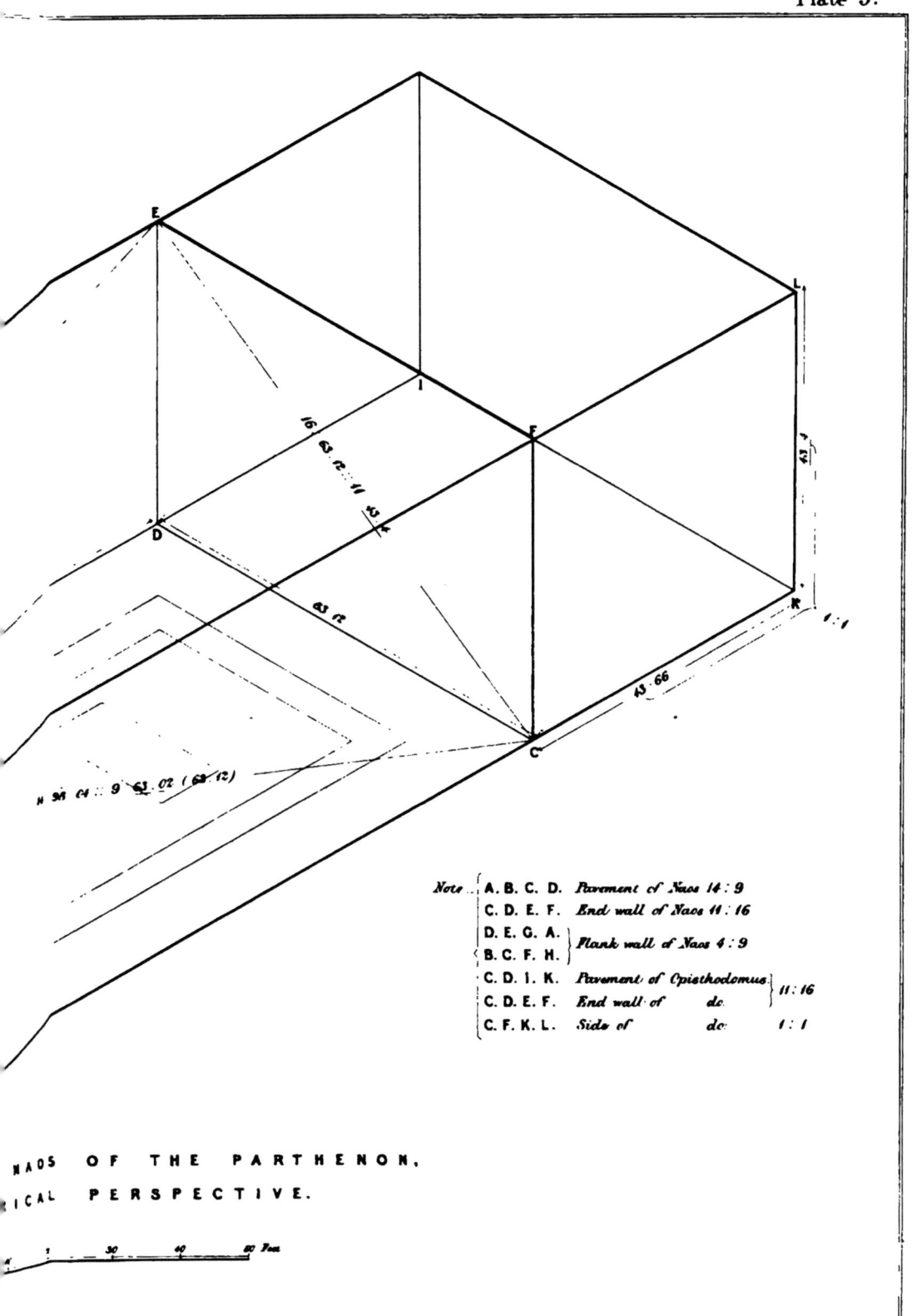

Note
- A. B. C. D. Pavement of Naos 14 : 9
- C. D. E. F. End wall of Naos 11 : 16
- D. E. G. A. } Flank wall of Naos 4 : 9
- B. C. F. H.
- C. D. I. K. Pavement of Opisthodomus } 11 : 16
- C. D. E. F. End wall of do.
- C. F. K. L. Side of do. 1 : 1

NAOS OF THE PARTHENON,
RICAL PERSPECTIVE.

Fig. 1.

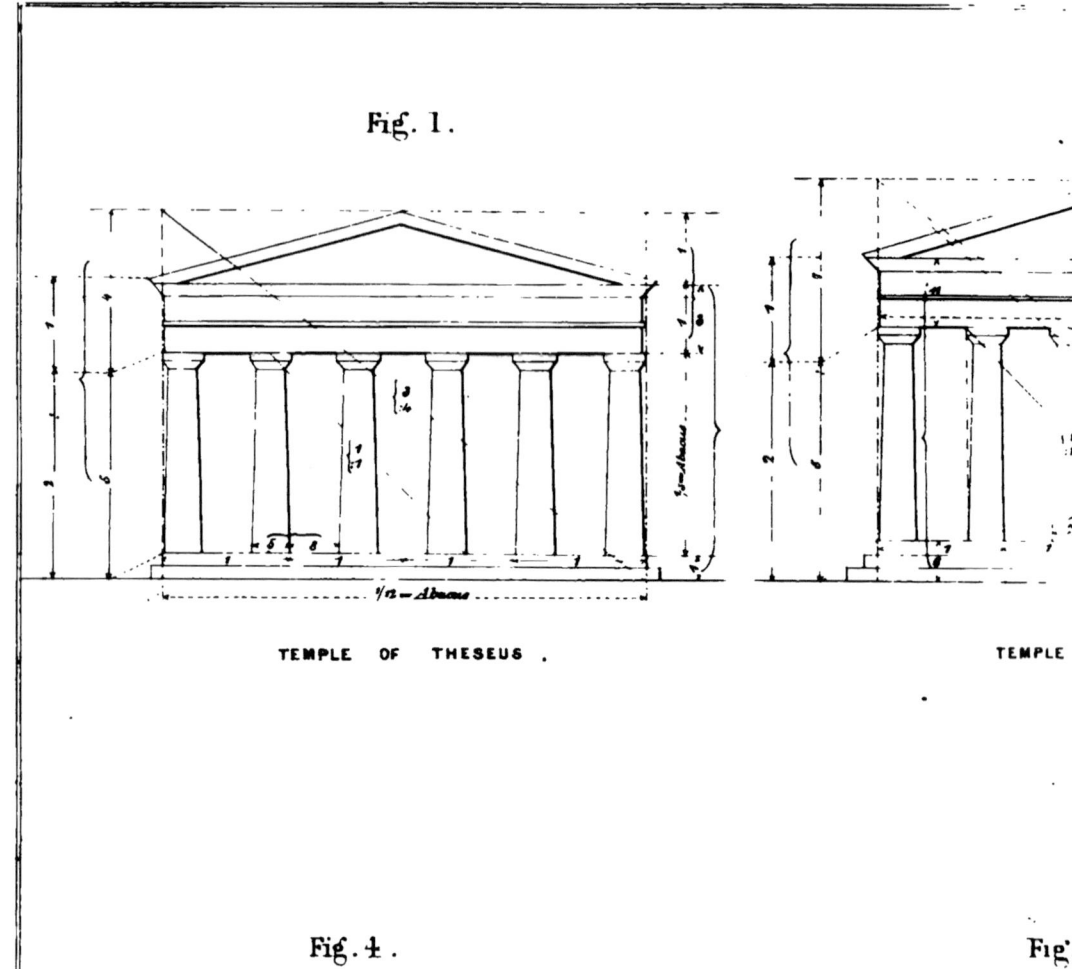

Fig. 4.

TEMPLE OF THESEUS.

TEMPLE

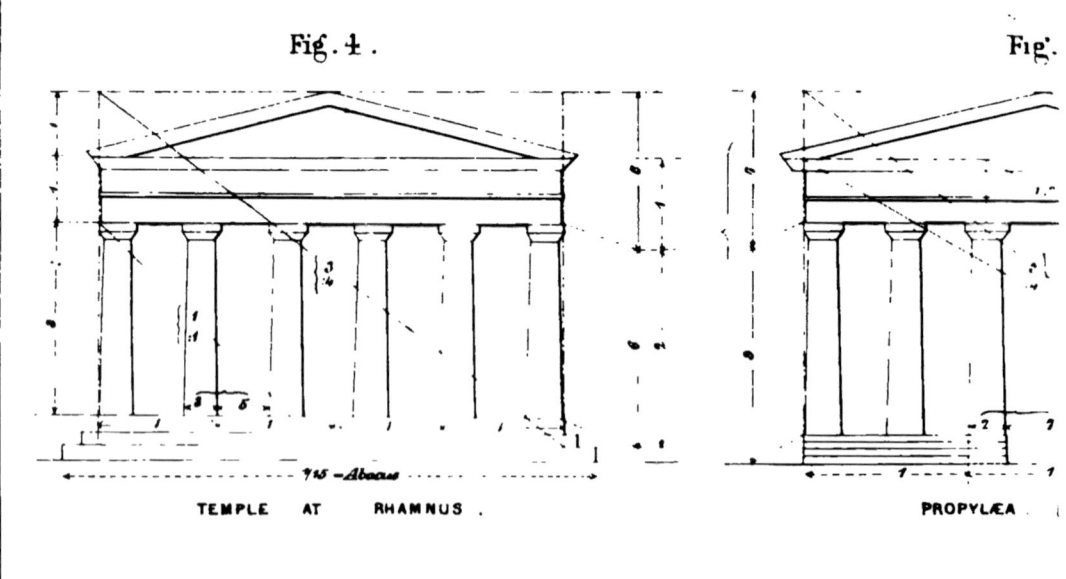

TEMPLE AT RHAMNUS.

PROPYLÆA

Fig.

SIX HEXASTYL

W. W. Lloyd, inven.

Plate 10

Fig. 2.

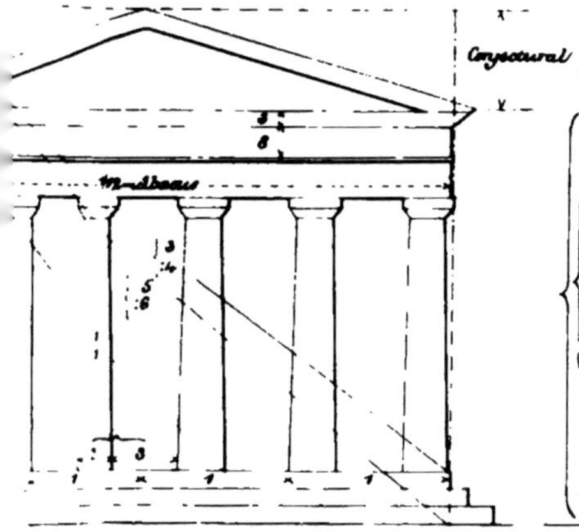

TEMPLE AT SUNIUM.

Fig. 3.

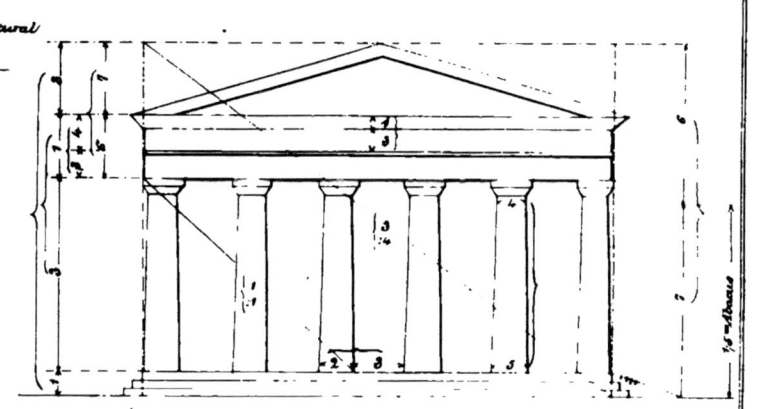

TEMPLE OF APOLLO
AT BASSÆ.

Fig. 5.

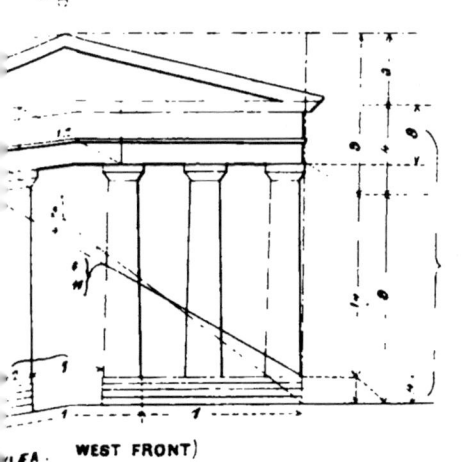

...LÆA. WEST FRONT)

Fig. 6.

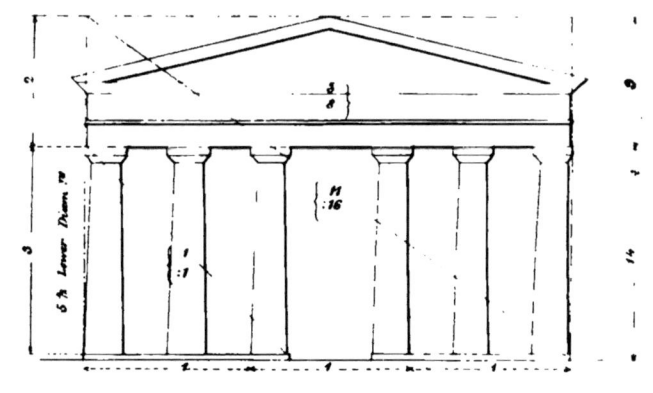

PROPYLÆA (EAST FRONT)

...ASTYLE PORTICOES.